KANJI
STARTER 2

KANJI
STARTER 2

Daiki Kusuya

Stone Bridge Press • Berkeley, California

Published by
Stone Bridge Press
P.O. Box 8208
Berkeley, CA 94707
TEL 510-524-8732 • sbp@stonebridge.com • www.stonebridge.com

First published by IBC Publishing, Tokyo, Japan. Reprinted by permission.

Printed in the United States of America.

2011 2010 2009 2008 2007 2006   10 9 8 7 6 5 4 3 2 1

CONTENTS

PREFACE

This book follows the same principle as the previous book, *Kanji Starter 1*—using pictographs and integrating characters to make kanji characters more easily recognizable.

The pictographs or ideas explaining kanji characters in this book are not necessarily based on their historical development. They may be alterations or even my own creations. The purpose of this book is to teach the meanings of kanji characters, not to show how they were derived.

DAIKI KUSUYA

SECTION 1

Excerpt from "Kanji Starter 1"

The following kanji characters are explained in the previous book, *Kanji Starter 1*. These are cited here for the purpose of explaining kanji characters newly appearing in this book.

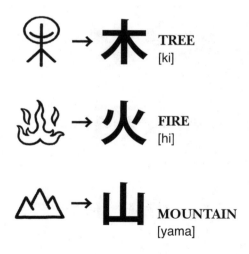

木 TREE
[ki]

火 FIRE
[hi]

山 MOUNTAIN
[yama]

 **VALLEY**
[tani]

area between
mountains

 **STONE**
[ishi]

cliff and a piece

 **WATER**
[mizu]

RAIN
[ame]

**SUN,
DAY**
[hi]

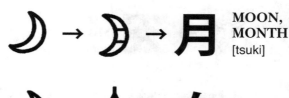 **MOON, MONTH** [tsuki]

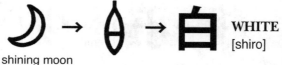 **WHITE** [shiro]

shining moon

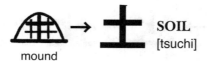 **SOIL** [tsuchi]

mound

 **GOLD, MONEY** [kin]

a mountain, soil and nuggets

 **PERSON** [hito]

 **HEAVEN, SKY** [ten]

supported by a gigantic person (like Atlas)

 **SMALL** [chī-sai] **LITTLE, LESS** [suku-nai]

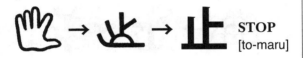 **STOP** [to-maru]

 **ENGINEERING** [kō]

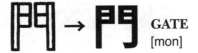 **GATE** [mon]

 **戸** DOOR
[to]

牛 COW
[ushi]

 **羊** SHEEP
[hitsuji]

馬 HORSE
[uma]

 **羽** WING, FEATHER
[hane]

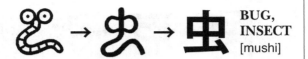 **BUG, INSECT** [mushi]

 **SHELL** [kai]

→ 目 **EYE** [me]

→ 見 **LOOK, WATCH** [mi-ru]

→ 耳 **EAR** [mimi]

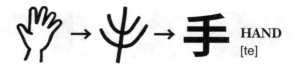 **HAND**
[te]

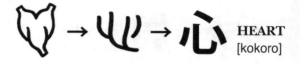 **HEART**
[kokoro]

 **MOUTH**
[kuchi]

 **SAY, TELL**
[i-u]

BOW
[yumi]

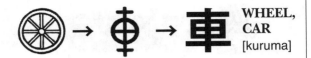 **WHEEL, CAR** [kuruma]

→ 竹 **BAMBOO** [take]

→ 糸 **THREAD** [ito]

→ 子 **CHILD** [ko]

relatively large head

 **STAND** [ta-tsu]

17

 **交** CROSS, EXCHANGE [maji-waru]

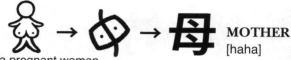 **母** MOTHER [haha]

a pregnant woman having large breasts

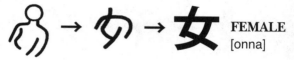 **女** FEMALE [onna]

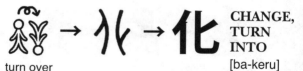 **化** CHANGE, TURN INTO [ba-keru]

turn over

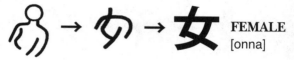 **冬** WINTER [fuyu]

wind and snow

$\bigwedge \rightarrow \bigwedge \rightarrow$ 力 **POWER, MIGHTY**
[chikara]

$\bigwedge \rightarrow$ 刀 **SWORD**
[katana]

$\bigwedge \rightarrow$ 斤 **HATCHET, AX**
[kin]

古 $\rightarrow$ 古 **OLD**
[furu-i]

ancient crown

固 $\rightarrow$ 固 **FIRM, SOLID**
[kata-i]

outer surface of
an old thing

19

One kanji character may be pronounced in different ways depending on how it is used. In SECTION 1 and SECTION 2, only one or two possible ways to pronounce the character are shown along with each character.

Numerals refer to the page on which the character was introduced.

stump

**ORIGIN,
BASIS**
[moto]

a fingerprint
for identity

**IDENTICAL,
THE SAME**
[ona-ji]

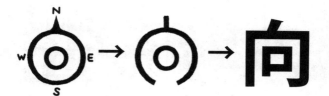

compass

**DIRECTION,
POINT
TOWARD**
[mu-ku]

**CIRCLE, YEN
(Japanese currency)**
[en]

22

左 → 左

LEFT
[hidari]

右 → 右

RIGHT
[migi]

→

hit the wall,
cannot go farther

UN-, DIS-
(makes negative
words)
[fu]

 →

13
stop a car exactly
at the line

RIGHT,
CORRECT,
PROPER
[tada-shii]

→

a house with a
long corridor

**WIDE, LARGE
(in terms of
space)**
[hiro-i]

 →

**LEAVE,
GO AWAY**
[sa-ru]

soapbox

**STAGE,
A STAND**
[dai]

**COMBINE,
FIT**
[a-u]

→

a table in a room

MEET
[a-u]

 →

an eye checking
time

NOW
[ima]

27

a spike making a …

HOLE
[ana]

① bull's-eye
② something *falls into* a category

HIT, FALL ON
[a-teru]
THIS, THE VERY
[tou]

14

N.Z., in the "south," is famous for **sheep**

SOUTH
[minami]

on the corner of a map

NORTH
[kita]

前 → 前 → **前**

head of an
animal

**BEFORE,
FRONT**
[mae]

 → **外**

the moon and the
door

OUTSIDE
[soto]

→

something
glittering deep in
a tunnel

**DEEP
INSIDE**
[oku]

 →

11

the sun rising
above the horizon

EARLY
[haya-i]

¹¹
the sun
comes up
over the
horizon

RISE
[nobo-ru]

FLY
[to-bu]

32

11, 12

sun rises between
grass (horizon)
while moon is
almost gone

MORNING
[asa]

a person
watching the
moon from
house

NIGHT
[yoru]

13

use two
hands on the
gate

OPEN
[a-keru]

 →

13

a hand and a bar

CLOSE
[shi-meru]

13

① mechanism to close a gate has closely connected parts
② the gate opens only for a person who has passed inspection

CONCERNED WITH, CLOSELY RELATED
[kaka-waru]
GATEWAY, CHECKPOINT
[kan]

two hooks

TO EACH OTHER, RECIPROCAL
[taga-i]

16

a decorated **bow** for a ceremony, not for practical use

WEAK
[yowa-i]

silk string (from silk **worm**) on a **bow**

15,16

STRONG
[tsuyo-i]

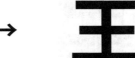

13

a person sent
from **heaven** to
the earth

KING
[ou]

the **king** under a
roof completely
rules all

**ALL,
COMPLETE**
[sube-te]

 →

① the **king** is at the center of everything
② the **main** person in a group

MAIN
[omo-na]
MASTER
[shu]

 →

in ancient times, the **king** was the only person who owned precious gems or pearls

BALL, PRECIOUS THING
[tama]

precious things
inside a border

→

COUNTRY
[kuni]

a mat on which a
person can lie

→

**BASED ON,
CAUSE**
[yo-ru]

→

the bridegroom
puts his hair up
with a pin in an
ancient wedding

HUSBAND
[otto]

 →

a **husband** was
hit by his wife
with a bat and fell
unconscious

**LOSE,
MISS**
[ushina-u]

18

mother pins up
her hair "every"
day

EVERY
[mai]

family genes

**YOUNGER
BROTHER**
[otōto]

 →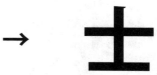

samurai warrior

**OFFICER,
WARRIOR**
[shi]

 →

two persons
side by side

COMPARE
[kura-beru]

→ 包

a person
crouching down,
covered with a
blanket

WRAP
[tsutsu-mu]

既 → 配

a person beside
a sake container,
serving sake

DISTRIBUTE
[kuba-ru]

43

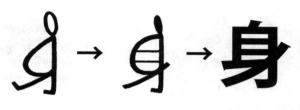

BODY
[mi]

SOUND
[oto]

→

easygoing juggler

**FUN,
EASY**
[raku]

a person with a
"full" stomach

**FULL,
FILL**
[jū]

育 → 育 → 育

a baby on a bed

**BRING UP,
REAR**
[soda-teru]

thumbs-up

GOOD
[yo-i]

46

 →

something good
like cake in a
mouth

EAT
[ta-beru]

 →

in ancient times,
people used their
fingers to eat

**MEAL,
COOKED RICE**
[meshi]

 →

a person with his
mouth open →
there is a space

欠

LACK
[ka-keru]

 →

① an officer calling…
② sequence

次

NEXT
[tsugi]
**(mathematical)
ORDER**
[ji]

48

 → →

**SHOUT,
SCREAM**
[sake-bu]

 → →

put an X mark
on the dead
person's chest for
protection from
bad spirits

**EVIL,
BAD LUCK**
[kyō]

a pattern on
the chest →
letters

**TEXT,
SENTENCE
(as in writing)**
[bun]

 →

SUPPORT
[sasa-eru]

→

17

threadlike lines
between skull
plates

THIN, SLIM
[hoso-i]
MINUTE, FINE
[koma-kai]

 →

16

in your mind and
in your **heart**

THINK OF
[omo-u]

in Japan, pointing
to one's nose
indicates "myself"

**SELF,
SPONTANEOUS**
[mizuka-ra]

BAD SMELL
[nio-u]

→

wrinkly face

GROW OLD
[o-iru]

 →

a wise old man
with a beard
contemplating

THINK
[kanga-eru]

NUMBERS

ONE
[ichi]

TWO
[ni]

THREE
[san]

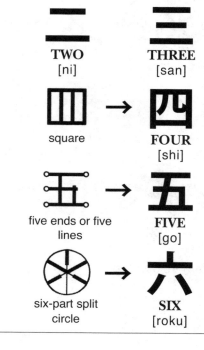

square → **FOUR** [shi]

five ends or five lines → **FIVE** [go]

six-part split circle → **SIX** [roku]

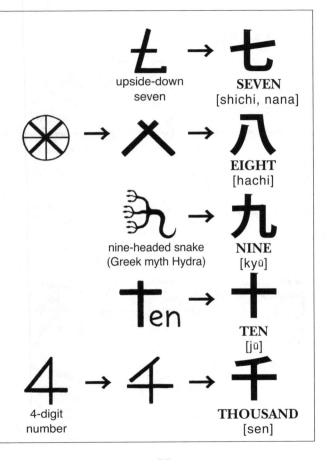

upside-down seven → **SEVEN** [shichi, nana]

→ × → **EIGHT** [hachi]

nine-headed snake (Greek myth Hydra) → **NINE** [kyū]

Ten → **TEN** [jū]

4-digit number → → **THOUSAND** [sen]

**BEAN,
PEA**
[mame]

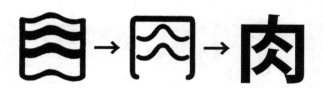

streaky
bacon

**MEAT,
FLESH**
[niku]

**WHEAT,
BARLEY**
[mugi]

the fibers of a
thread

**ELEMENT,
ORIGINAL,
PLAIN**
[moto]

17

a **thread** is
connected to
another thread

SOMETHING
RELATED,
SYSTEM,
LINEAGE
[kei]

a watermelon
sliced open

FRUIT,
ESSENCE,
SUBSTANTIAL
[mi]

HORN
[tsuno]
CORNER
[kado]

**SHELL (of turtle),
BACK OF THE
HAND**
[kō]

FANG
[kiba]

**a counter for
animals**
[hiki, piki,
biki]

→

young leafy plant
later **changes**
into…

FLOWER
[hana]

 →

flower
arrangement

ART
[gei]

→

a smelly colony in
a petri dish

**GERM,
FUNGUS**
[kin]

branch of a
tree

**GENERATION,
GENERAL PUBLIC,
WORLD**
[se, yo]

 →

10

a **tree** with many
branches

LEAF
[ha]

① flag indicating that "market"
is open
② area that grows around the
market

MARKET
[ichi]
CITY
[shi]

63

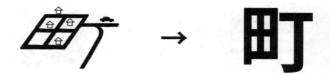

→ 町

TOWN
(administrative)
[machi]

衚 → 街 → 街

many streets

CITY
(a hectic area /
street)
[machi]

→

separated areas
by borders

**DISTRICT,
WARD**
[ku]

 →

building with
a bell hanging
inside

TEMPLE
[tera]

→

place where one
can relax

**HOUSE,
HOME**
[ie]

 →

building with shelf
and display case

**SHOP,
STORE**
[mise]

SEAT
[seki]

14

a **horse** is hitched
to a post

STATION
[eki]

→

a house with a
big container full
of rice

**RICH,
WEALTH**
[tomi]

**CLOTHES,
DRESS**
[koromo]

**HANG,
SUSPEND**
[tsuru-su]

 →

atomizer

**FRAGRANCE,
SCENT**
[kao-ri]

hourglass

**USED UP,
RUN OUT**
[tsu-kiru]

scales

**MEASURE,
PLOT**
[haka-ru]

→

weight of piled
books

HEAVY
[omo-i]
HEAP UP
[kasa-neru]

books on a shelf

VOLUME
[satsu]

→

① displayed cans
② the value of an
article

**GOODS,
ARTICLE**
[shina]

QUALITY
[hin]

a container
with a pop-top

CAN
[kan]

 →

STRIKE, HIT
[u-tsu]

 →

15

knife used to
open a **clam**

**MEANS FOR WORK,
IMPLEMENT**
[gu]

→

attaché case

**COMMERCE,
DO BUSINESS**
[akina-u]

① a frame
② a design

**PICTURE,
DRAWING**
[ga]

DRAW UP A PLAN
[kaku]

 →

**IGNITE,
POINT, DOT**
[tsu-keru]

 →

**SHINE,
ILLUMINATE**
[te-rasu]

COLORS

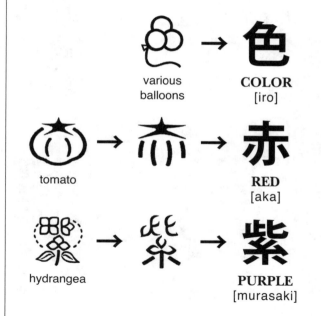

various balloons → 色
COLOR
[iro]

tomato → 亦 → 赤
RED
[aka]

hydrangea → 紫 → 紫
PURPLE
[murasaki]

dandelion → **黄**
YELLOW
[ki]

① color of soil
② **brown** beverage

BROWN [cha]
TEA [cha]

grasshopper → **緑**
GREEN
[midori]

beyond the palm trees are
the blue sea and the blue
sky

BLUE
[ao]

12

→

a part of the plant
that pushes leaves
up from the *ground*
like an arm does

**STEM,
STALK**
[kuki]

17, 12

→

a **car** that can be
lifted up from the
ground by hand
is…

LIGHT
[karu-i]

98

to hand
something to a
person

**ADD,
GIVE**
[tsu-keru]

a gem in the hand
and the house

PROTECT
[mamo-ru]

→

16

hand holding a stick, chanting
mouth → chief of the tribe
who uses witchcraft

**LORD
(archaic), YOU
(contemporary)**
[kimi]

 → 名

16

the first thing you
say when you
meet a person for
the first time

NAME
[na]

80

→

in ancient times,
a warrior cut off
his enemy's ear
(as proof of his
victory)

**TAKE,
GET**
[to-ru]

 →

a hand on the
wall of the prison
pushing against
boundaries

**OPPOSE,
AGAINST**
[han]

→

**CLOTH,
SPREAD**
[nuno]

 →

① uncommon **cloth**
② **rare**, hard to obtain

RARE
[mare]
HOPE
[ki]

→

something peeled
using a hand

**SKIN (noun),
HIDE (noun)**
[kawa]

 →

hand to hand

**RECEIVE,
TAKE**
[u-keru]

→

hand in hand

FRIEND
[tomo]

 → 援

99

hands surrounding a **friend** (or simply, "4 hands")

HELP, SUPPORT
[en]

84

11

put a coat on a
friend's shoulder to
make the person
"warm," like the
sun does

→

WARM
[atata-kai]

16

→

**RAISE TO
SHOW, CITE**
[a-geru]

 →

**DEMON,
OGRE**
[oni]

 → 死

ash/cinder under
ground (Japanese
custom)

DEATH
[shi]

→

death penalty

**CRIME,
GUILT**
[tsumi]

 →

alien

**DIFFER,
FOREIGN**
[koto-naru]

→

a group of people
heading for the
castle

SOLDIER
[hei]

 →

a villain in jail with
evil in his **heart**

BAD
[waru-i]

→

16

having something
strongly in one's
heart

**ABSOLUTE,
WITHOUT
FAIL**
[kanara-zu]

 →

16

a hand grabs a
diamond someone
loves in a…

**HURRY,
URGENT**
[isogu]

怒 → 怒 → 怒

16

state of **heart**
that makes
angry eyes

GET ANGRY
[oko-ru]

努 → 努 → 努

19

exerting great
force

**ENDEAVOR,
EFFORT**
[tsuto-meru]

① view from the window
② there is nothing in the **sky**

SKY
[sora]
EMPTY
[kara]

migrating
birds stop by
mountains in
the ocean

ISLAND
[shima]

11

→

rain and a turbine make…

ELECTRIC
[den]

11

one form of **rain** that looks like a feather

SNOW
[yuki]

¹¹
mass that
brings **rain**

CLOUD
[kumo]

energy
emanating
from the core

**GAS,
MOOD,
SPIRIT**
[ki]

93

池 → 池 → 池

boat, oar, and
water

POND

[ike]

soil by **pond**   →   地

12

**GROUND,
PLACE**

[chi]

94

SECTION 2

Boldface type in small letters indicates that the translation was introduced in SECTION 1 or immediately before.

Italic type indicates the extended translation, adapted from the original translation in SECTION 1.

Numerals refer to the page on which the character/component was introduced.

COMPONENTS

Following are some components used in kanji characters. The meanings shown along with each component may not be the original (historical) ones and may have been altered somewhat so that the kanji character can be easily understood. They are not individual kanji characters and thus do not have a pronuniciation.

COMPONENTS

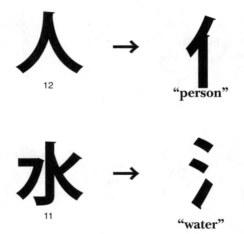

人
12

→

亻
"person"

水
11

→

氵
"water"

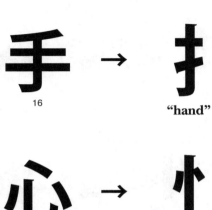

手 → 扌

16

"hand"

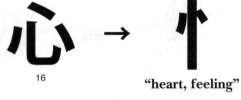

心 → 忄

16

"heart, feeling"

广

"building, roof"

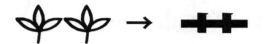

"plants"

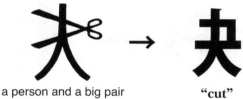

a person and a big pair
of scissors

"cut"

12

"moon" /
"meat, body part"
(the latter is derived from 肉 → p.56)

欠 → 欠

"lack, open, open-mouthed"

48

貝 → 貝

"shell, money, valuable things"

15

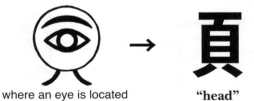 → 頁

where an eye is located → "head"

boxes stacked one on
top of another

"pile up"

53

"old person"

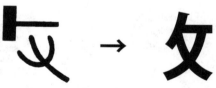

a hammer in a hand

"beat"

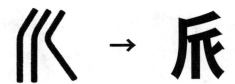

"stream that
divides"

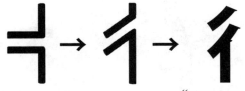

"street corner,
go"

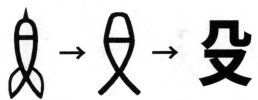

dart

"weapon for
throwing, go far"

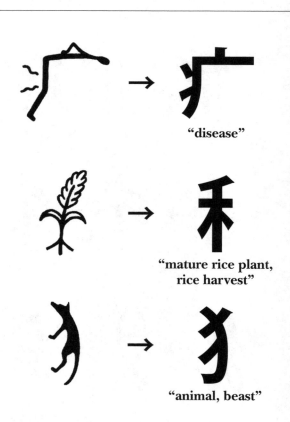

"disease"

"mature rice plant,
rice harvest"

"animal, beast"

→

a man pressed from
sides

"pinch, narrow"

82

→

"cloth"

68

→

"wealth"

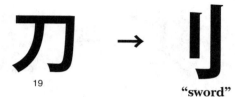

刀 → リ

₁₉

"sword"

① the sun setting between plants
(horizon), getting dark, the sun is…
② feel for something not seen
(because covered)

→ 莫

"covered"
"look for"

① town square
② along the perimeter

"square"
"lap, cycle"

"street, road"

"bird"

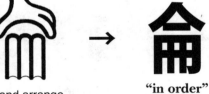

gather and arrange books

"in order"

宀 99 **+** **元** 21 **→** **完**

the **foundation** of a **house** should be…

PERFECT, COMPLETE, FINISH
[kan]

宀 99 **+** **子** 17 **→** **字**

a **child** in a **house** is not playing but writing…

LETTERS (as those in words)
[ji]

宀 99 **+** **女** 18 **→** **安**

① when a **woman** is there, **home** is…
② a **woman** tries to manage the *family* budget

SAFE
[an]
CHEAP
[yasu-i]

108

広 + 木 → 床

the **wood** under a **roof**

FLOOR
[yuka]

広+人+人+土→ 座

people on the *ground* under the **roof**

SIT,
SEAT
[suwa-ru]

金 + 同 → 銅

looks *similar* to **gold**

COPPER
[dō]

竹 + 同 → 筒

17   21

a hollow cylinder *just like*
bamboo

TUBE
[tsutsu]

不 + 口 → 否

24   16

**DENIAL,
SAY NO**
[hi]

口 + 土 → 吐

16   12

from the **mouth** to
the *ground*

**PUSH OUT FROM
MOUTH (SPIT, VOMIT,
EXHALE)**
[ha-ku]

言 + 正 → 証
16   24

the *words* are **right**

**PROOF,
EVIDENCE**
[akashi]

手 + 広 → 拡
99   25

a **hand** *rolls out* pizza dough

**SPREAD,
ENLARGE**
[kaku]

金 + 広 → 鉱
12   25

search for **gold** in a **big** space

MINING
[kō]

水 + 台 → 治

98   26

water behind a *dam*

GOVERN
[osa-meru]
RECOVER
[nao-ru]

女 + 台 → 始

18   26

a **woman** on a **stage** will
"begin" to sing

BEGIN
[haji-meru]

手 + 穴 + 木 → 探

99   28   10

with your **hand** in a **hole**
in a **tree**

SEARCH
[saga-su]

水 + 穴 + 木 → 深
98   28   10

the **water** in the **hole** in the **tree** is…

DEEP
[fuka-i]

水 + 夜 → 液
98   33

dew forms at **night**

LIQUID
[eki]

艹 + 早 → 草
100   31

early stage of **plant** (without a flower)

GRASS
[kusa]

herbal formula to regain health
and *happy feeling*

MEDICINE
[kusuri]

① tea made from **old herbs**
tastes…
② and to drink it all is…

BITTER
[niga-i]
PAINFUL

人 + 固 → 個
98   19

the **person** has a **solidly**
established character

木 + 主 → 柱
10   38

the **main** piece of **wood** that holds up the roof

PILLAR, POST
[hashira]

人 + 主 → 住
98   38

the **main** place a **person** stays is their home

LIVE IN
[su-mu]

水 + 毎 → 海
98   41

water is *everywhere*

SEA
[umi]

心 + 毎 → 悔
99   41

a **feeling** that one has **every**
time after a mistake

REGRET
[kuya-mu]

心 + 夬 → 快
99   100

the **feeling** when all your
worries are **cut** away

**PLEASANT,
FINE**
[kokoroyo-i]

水 + 夬 → 決
98   100

sweating while "deciding" which
wire to **cut** to defuse the bomb

DECIDE
[ki-meru]

when you **compare white** things, all are the same color

ALL, EVERYONE
[mina]

quill pen and **blank** paper for studying

PRACTICE, LEARN
[nara-u]

音 + 心 → 意
44　　16

sound (words) from the **heart**

WILL, MIND
[i]

土 + 音 + 人 → 境

12   44   12

① the *land* limit where *citizens* can go or *speak* freely
② the **border** is fixed under certain conditions

BORDER
[sakai]
SITUATION
[kyou]

金 + 音 + 人 → 鏡

12   44   12

metal that can reflect **sound** or a **human** figure

MIRROR
[kagami]

金 + 充 → 銃

12   45

loading *metal* balls into a…

GUN
[jū]

金 ₁₂ + 良 ₄₆ → 銀

the next **best** *metal* to gold

SILVER
[gin]

女 ₁₈ + 良 ₄₆ → 娘

DAUGHTER, GIRL
[musume]

羊 ₁₄ + 食 ₄₇ → 養

raise a **sheep** for *food*

REAR, FOSTER
[yashina-u]

食 + 包 → 飽

food **wrapped** in a stomach

SATIATED, SATURATED
[a-kiru]

月 + 包 → 胞

biological **wrapping**

MEMBRANE SACK
[hō]

手 + 包 → 抱

arms wrapping something

HOLD SOMETHING IN ARMS, EMBRACE
[da-ku]

水 + 包 → 泡
98   43

water wrapping air

BUBBLE,
FOAM
[awa]

石 + 包 → 砲
11   43

barrel in which a **stone** bullet is
wrapped (held)

CANNON,
GUN
[hō]

口 + 欠 → 吹
16   101

BLOW
[fu-ku]

火 + 欠 → 炊
10   101

blow on a **fire** to make the fire
bigger to…

COOK

[ta-ku]

食 + 欠 → 飲
47   101

eating without this **lacks**
something

DRINK

[no-mu]

谷 + 欠 → 欲
11   101

a feeling of **lacking**, like a
valley which will never be filled

**DESIRE,
WANT**

[yoku]

水 + 谷 → 浴

98　　11

a clean *river* runs into a
valley and one wants to…

BATHE
[a-biru]

次 + 貝 → 資

48　　101

① the **next** project needs **money**
② something to be *based on*

FUNDS
[shi]

MATERIAL

化 + 貝 → 貨

18　　101

① **sea shell exchangeable** for
other things (in ancient times)
② things that can be bought with
money

MONEY
[ka]

COMMODITY
[ka]

123

化 + 頁 → 傾

18   101

change the position of one's **head**

TILT, IMBALANCED
[katamu-ku]

火 + 頁 → 煩

10   101

a *hot* **head** is…

BOTHERSOME, ANNOYING
[wazura-washii]

貝 + 曽 → 贈

101   102

catch a **pile** of **clams** and give them to someone

PRESENT
[oku-ru]

124

pile up some **soil**

INCREASE
[fu-eru]

feeling that **piles up**

HATE
[niku-mu]

木 + 支 → 枝

10   50

supportive (not main) part of a **tree**

BRANCH
[eda]

125

手 + 支 → 技
99   50

using **hands** to **support**
one's career

**SKILL,
TECHNIQUE**
[waza]

月 + 支 → 肢
100   50

supportive part of the **body**

LIMB
[shi]

自 + 心 → 息
52   16

to make the **heart** beat and to
keep **oneself** alive

BREATH
[iki]

126

102 11

the nature of a human being is
to get **older** day by day

PERSON
[mono]

日 + 者 → 暑

11 127

a **person** under the **sun** feels…

HOT
(as in weather)
[atsu-i]

歨 + 子 → 孝

102 17

the feeling of **children** for their
parents

FILIAL
PIETY
[kō]

孝 + 攵 → 教
127 102

a parent **spanks** a child to
teach him/her a *lesson*

TEACH
[oshi-eru]

貝 + 攵 → 敗
101 102

money lost through being
beaten

**DEFEATED,
LOSE**
[yabu-reru]

正 + 攵 → 政
24 102

the **correct** use of *force*

POLITICS
[sei]

128

木 + 攵 → 枚

10   102

wood is **beaten** into pulp to
make paper

**SHEET OF
(a counter)**
[mai]

牛 + 攵 → 牧

14   102

cows driven by **beating**

**STOCK FARM,
RAISE LIVESTOCK**
[boku]

工 + 攵 → 攻

13   102

beat with *tools*

ATTACK
[se-meru]

工 + 力 → 功

13   19

engineering (tool) and **power**

ACHIEVEMENT
[kō]

月 + 厎 → 脈

100   103

dividing stream running in the **body**

(BLOOD) STREAM, PULSE
[myaku]

水 + 厎 → 派

98   103

water/things *separated from* the main body

DERIVATIVE, SECT
[ha]

人 + 系 → 係
98   58

the key **person** in a
system

**A PERSON IN CHARGE,
CONCERNED WITH**
[kakari]

子 + 系 → 孫
17   58

child in a **lineage**

GRANDCHILD
[mago]

糸 + 冬 → 終
17   18

when icicles melt and become
thin like **thread**, the **winter**
comes to an…

END
[o-waru]

131

角 + 虫 → 触

59　　15

a **horn** is used by **insects**

TOUCH
[sawa-ru]

角 + 刀 + 牛 → 解

59　19　14

① *cut* **horns** off a **cow**
② **break up** and look at details
to know things

BREAK UP, UNDO
[to-ku]
COMPREHEND
[kai]

手 + 甲 → 押

99　　59

using your **hand** and seeing the
back of your hand when you
open a door

PUSH
[o-su]

132

女 + **市** → **姉**
18　　63

female member of a family who
goes to **market** often

ELDER
SISTER
[ane]

馬 + **区** → **駆**
14　　65

horses were used to
communicate between
wards

RUN, DRIVE
SOMETHING INTO
[ka-keru]

日 + **寺** → **時**
11　　65

during the **day** the **temple** bell
rings to tell the…

TIME,
HOUR
[toki, ji]

133

牛 + 寺 → 特
14　　65

a **cow** offered to a **temple**

SPECIAL
[toku]

竹 + 寺 → 等
17　　65

① **bamboo** used to make the
fence of a **temple** all has the same
length
② things are **equal** only in the same…

EQUAL
[hito-shii]
RANK
[tou]

言 + 寺 → 詩
16　　65

(originally) *words* dedicated to
God at a **temple**

POETRY
[shi]

人 + 寺 → 侍
98   65

a *guardian* of a **temple**

SAMURAI
[samurai]

亻 + 寺 → 待
103   65

everyone meets at
the **temple** on the
corner

WAIT
[ma-tsu]
TO RECEIVE A PERSON
[tai]

亻 + 殳 → 役
103   103

go with a **weapon** for
military duty

DUTY,
ROLE
[yaku]

手 + 殳 → 投

99   103

a **hand** with a **weapon** will…

THROW
[na-geru]

水 + 殳 → 没

98   103

a **weapon** thrown into **water** will…

SINK
[botsu]

車 + 殳 + 手 → 撃

17   103   16

from a **car** a **weapon** is *thrown*

ATTACK, SHOOT
[u-tsu]

疒 + 殳 → 疫

₁₀₄　　₁₀₃

widely thrown (spread)
disease

PLAGUE
[eki]

女 + 家 → 嫁

₁₈　　₆₆

a **woman** joining a *family*

BRIDE, WIFE
[yome]

人 + 衣 → 依

₉₈　　₆₈

a **person** pulling another
person's *sleeve*

**RELY ON,
DEPENDENT ON**
[yo-ru]

重 + **力** → **動**
71   19

a **heavy** thing has **power**
applied to it

MOVE
[ugo-ku]

人 + **動** → **働**
98   138

a **person moving**

WORK
[hatara-ku]

禾 + **重** → **種**
104   71

① the head of a **rice plant**
   becomes **heavy** with…
② a group from the same **seed**,
   different from other groups

SEED
[tane]

KIND, SORT
[shu]

138

the **rice harvest** is the means
by which a *family* lives

EARN

[kase-gu]

season of **harvest** and **fire-**
colored leaves

AUTUMN

[aki]

禾 + 口 → 和

104   16

harvested rice in the **mouth**
gives one

**COMFORT,
HARMONY**

[nago-mu]

禾 (104) **+** **子** (17) **→** **季**

a *rice-stalk* hat on a **child**
(for a harvest festival)

SEASON
[ki]

禾 (104) **+** **少** (13) **→** **秒**

tiny amount of **rice harvest** →
tiny amount

SECOND
(unit of time)
[byō]

止 (13) **+** **少** (13) **→** **歩**

the best way to move if you
need to make *small* **stops**

WALK
[aru-ku]

木 10 + 交 18 → 校

a building with **crossed timbers**
→ a large wooden building

SCHOOL
[kō]

羽 14 + 異 87 → 翼

many **feathers** have a **different**
function

WING
[tsubasa]

水 98 + 兵 88 → 浜

water brings **soldiers** to the…

BEACH,
SHORE
[hama]

君 + 羊 → 群
80   14

a **lord** who owns **sheep** has a
herd of them

**GROUP,
HERD**
[mure]

犭 + 守 → 狩
104   79

kill **beasts** to **protect** human
lives

HUNT
[ka-ru]

犭 + 夹 → 狭
104   105

path made by **animals** *wedging*
their ways through

NARROW
[sema-i]

手 + 夹 → 挟
99   105

a **hand** making something
narrow

PINCH
[hasa-mu]

山 + 夹 → 峡
10   105

mountains pressing in on the
sides

CANYON
[kyō]

布 + 日 + 目 → 帽
105   11   15

a thing made of **fabric** for
protecting **eyes** from the **sun**

HAT, CAP
[bō]

143

手 + 目 → 看

16   15

hands and **eyes** working
on a thing

LOOK CAREFULLY,
LOOK AFTER
[mi-ru]

布 + 富 → 幅

105   105

a large **expensive** piece of
cloth

WIDTH
[haba]

富 + リ → 副

105   106

wealth *divided*

SUB-
[fuku]

莫 + 布 → 幕
106   105

cloth covering the stage

CURTAIN,
SHROUD
[maku]

莫 + 力 → 募
106   19

look for powers

RECRUIT,
COLLECT
[tsuno-ru]

莫 + 日 → 暮
106   11

① the **sun** is *gone*, the
day is over
② spend days

COME TO AN END
[ku-reru]

TO LIVE
[ku-rasu]

月 + 莫 → 膜
100   106

a *biological* **covering** or film

MEMBRANE
[maku]

莫 + 土 → 墓
106   12

a dead body **covered** by **soil** is in a…

GRAVE, TOMB
[haka]

其 + 土 → 基
106   12

the foundation of a house is in a **square** hole in the **ground**

BASIS
[moto]

其 + 月 → 期
106   100

a **lunar cycle**

**PERIOD (of time),
TERM, STAGE**
[ki]

土 + 反 → 坂
12   81

to go up a *hill* you have to *fight*
gravity

SLOPE
[saka]

木 + 反 → 板
10   81

against the natural form of the
tree

BOARD
[ita]

貝 + **反** → **販**
101   81

money *comes and goes*

SALE
[han]

辶 + **反** → **返**
107   81

opposite way, **way back**

RETURN
[kae-ru]

辶 + **車** → **連**
107   17

an endless line of **cars** on a **highway**

CONTINUAL
[tsura-naru]

辶 + 隹 → 進
107　107

birds fly on a migratory **route**

PROCEED,
ADVANCE
[susu-mu]

辶 + 斤 → 近
107　19

cut a short **path** through the woods

NEAR,
CLOSE
[chika-i]

戸 + 斤 → 所
14　19

the proper "place" for a fire **ax** is behind a glass **door**

PLACE
[tokoro]

立 + 木 + 斤 → 新
17   10   19

a **standing tree** is cut with an
ax to make a "new" house

NEW
[atara-shii]

立 + 木 + 見 → 親
17   10   15

a person to be **looked** up to like
a **standing tree**

PARENT
[oya]

INTIMATE
[shita-shii]

水 + 皮 → 波
98   83

the *surface* of the *sea*

WAVE
[nami]

石 + 皮 → 破

11   83

work on a **hide** with a **stone**

TEAR, BREAK

[yabu-ru]

手 + 受 → 授

99   83

GIVE, GRANT

[sazu-keru]

三 + 人 + 日 → 春

54   12   11

three people lying under the **sun**

SPRING (season)

[haru]

七 + 刀 → 切

55   19

separate into **seven** pieces with
a **sword**

CUT
[ki-ru]

九 + 木 + 隹 → 雑

55   10   107

in **nine trees**, various kinds
of **birds** resting

MISCELLANEOUS
[zatsu]

水 + 九 + 木 → 染

98   55   10

use **nine** *liquids* obtained from
trees

DYE
[so-meru]

石 + 九 + 十 → 砕

11　　55　　55

break a **stone** into **nine** or **ten** pieces

CRUSH
[kuda-ku]

十 + 具 → 真

55　　73

something hidden that required **ten** *tools* to reveal

TRUTH, GENUINE
[shin]

水 + 青 → 清

98　　77

the **blue** *sea* is…

CLEAN
[kiyo-i]

日 + 青 → 晴

11   77

sun and **blue** sky

**FINE
WEATHER**
[ha-re]

心 + 青 → 情

99   77

clear **heart**, *pure* **feeling**

**SYMPATHY,
EMOTION**
[jou]

言 + 青 → 請

16   77

talk to the **blue** sky (heaven)

REQUEST
[ko-u]

154

言 + 侖 → 論
16   107

words in a carefully considered
order

ARGUE,
THEORY
[ron-jiru]

人 + 侖 → 倫
98   107

people having *proper relations*

ETHICS
[rin]

耳 + 心 → 恥
15   16

ears revealing **feelings**
(by turning red)

EMBARRASSMENT,
SHAME
[haji]

155

SECTION 3

COMBINATION
of two or more characters

 [ganjitsu]	(the **day** a year *starts*) ↓ **NEW YEAR'S DAY**	21, 11
 [dōjitsu]	**(ON THE) SAME DAY**	21, 11
 [dōitsu]	**SAMENESS, IDENTICALNESS**	21, 54
[keikō]	**TENDENCY**	124, 22
 [hidarite]	**LEFT HAND, ON THE LEFT**	23, 16

 **RIGHT HAND, ON THE RIGHT**

[migite] 23, 16

 **ILLICITNESS, INJUSTICE**

[fusei] 24, 24

 **NATIONAL DIET**

[kokkai] 39, 27

 TODAY

[kyō] 27, 11

 THIS MONTH

[kongetsu] 27, 12

当日 [tōjitsu]	**ON THAT DAY** 28, 11
正当 [seitō]	(**hit** the *point*) ↓ **JUSTNESS, RIGHTEOUSNESS** 24, 28
不当 [futō]	**UNJUSTNESS,** **UNFAIRNESS** 24, 28
交互 [kōgo]	**ALTERNATE** 18, 35
前日 [zenjitsu]	**PREVIOUS DAY,** **THE DAY BEFORE** 30, 11

駅前 [ekimae]	**IN FRONT OF THE STATION**	67, 30
外車 [gaisha]	**IMPORTED CAR**	30, 17
外交 [gaikō]	**DIPLOMACY**	30, 18
今朝 [kesa]	**THIS MORNING**	27, 33
今夜 [kon-ya]	**TONIGHT**	27, 33

深夜 [shin-ya]	**LATE AT NIGHT, MIDNIGHT** 113, 33
関係 [kankei]	**RELATIONSHIP** 35, 131
関心 [kanshin]	**INTEREST** 35, 16
強弱 [kyōjaku]	**STRONG AND WEAK** 36, 36
強力 [kyōryoku]	**POWERFUL, MIGHT** 36, 19

安全 [anzen]	(no anxiety, **completely safe**) ↓ **SAFETY** 108, 37
完全 [kanzen]	**PERFECT** 108, 37
全力 [zenryoku]	**AT FULL POWER, WITH UTMOST EFFORT** 37, 19
家主 [yanushi]	**LANDLORD** 66, 38
国家 [kokka]	**NATION** 39, 66

外国 [gaikoku]	**FOREIGN COUNTRY** 30, 39	

外国人 [gaikokujin]	**FOREIGNER** 30, 39, 12	

全国 [zenkoku]	**WHOLE COUNTRY** 37, 39	

夫人 [fujin]	(the **person** with a **husband**) ↓ **WIFE** 40, 12	

毎日 [mainichi]	**EVERY DAY** 40, 11	

小包 [kozutsumi]	**PARCEL** 13, 43	
手配 [tehai]	**ARRANGEMENT** 16, 43	
全身 [zenshin]	**WHOLE BODY** 37, 44	
自身 [jishin]	**ONESELF** 52, 44	
音楽 [ongaku]	**MUSIC** 44, 45	

教育 [kyōiku]	**EDUCATION**	128, 46
不良 [furyō]	**BADNESS, DELINQUENT**	24, 46
良心 [ryōshin]	**CONSCIENCE**	46, 16
朝食 [chōshoku]	**BREAKFAST**	33, 47
外食 [gaishoku]	**EATING OUT**	30, 47

一次 [ichiji]	**FIRST ORDER, PRIMARY** 54, 48
論文 [ronbun]	**THESIS** 155, 50
文化 [bunka]	(the result of *developed* **writing**, i.e. knowledge) ↓ **CULTURE** 50, 18
思考 [shikō]	**THINKING** 51, 53
自立 [jiritsu]	**SELF-SUSTAINING, INDEPENDENCE** 52, 17

老人
[rōjin]

OLD PERSON

53, 12

牛肉
[gyūniku]

BEEF

14, 56

皮肉
[hiniku]

(bitter comment that penetrates
skin and reaches inside the **body**)
↓
IRONY

83, 56

小麦
[komugi]

WHEAT

13, 57

元素
[genso]

ATOMIC ELEMENT

21, 57

真実 [shinjitsu]	**TRUTH** 153, 58
実力 [jitsuryoku]	**REAL ABILITY** 58, 19
三角 [sankaku]	**TRIANGLE** 54, 59
花火 [hanabi]	**FIREWORKS** 61, 10
雑草 [zassō]	**WEED** 152, 113

海草 [kaisō]	**SEAWEED**	115, 113
投薬 [tōyaku]	**ADMINISTERING A DRUG**	136, 114
文芸 [bungei]	**LITERATURE**	50, 51
細菌 [saikin]	**GERM, BACTERIA**	51, 62
市街地 [shigaichi]	**URBAN DISTRICT**	63, 64, 94

商店街
[shōtengai]

SHOPPING STREET

74, 66, 64

地区
[chiku]

DISTRICT

94, 65

音楽家
[ongakuka]

("music"+ a family
business run at **home**)
↓
MUSICIAN

44, 45, 66

画家
[gaka]

PAINTER

74, 66

開店
[kaiten]

OPENING A SHOP

34, 66

支店 [shiten]	(a secondary **store** *away from the main* store) ↓ **BRANCH STORE** 50, 66
欠席 [kesseki]	**ABSENCE** 48, 67
座席 [zaseki]	**SEAT** 109, 67
空席 [kūseki]	**VACANT SEAT** 91, 67
香水 [kōsui]	**PERFUME** 69, 11

 **CLOCK, WATCH**

[tokei]　　133, 70

 **TOTAL**

[gōkei]　　26, 70

会計 **ACCOUNT, RECEIPT**
(at restaurants)

[kaikei]　　27, 70

 **DOUBLE, OVERLAP**

[nijū]　　54, 71

 GRAVITY

[jūryoku]　　71, 19

 **COMMERCIAL GOODS, COMMODITIES**

[shōhin] 74, 72

 **FOOD PRODUCT**

[shokuhin] 47, 72

 **MEDICINE, A PHARMACEUTICAL**

[yakuhin] 114, 72

 **FURNITURE**

[kagu] 66, 73

 **STATIONERY**

[bungu] 50, 73

区画 [kukaku]	(*area* separated by *line*) ↓ **COMPARTMENT, ZONE** 65, 74
計画 [keikaku]	**PLAN** 70, 74
欠点 [ketten]	**DEFECT** 48, 75
重点 [jūten]	**EMPHASIS, FOCUS** 71, 75
終点 [shūten]	**TERMINAL, LAST STOP** 131, 75

悪人 [akunin]	**EVIL MAN, WICKED MAN** 88, 12	
悪化 [akka]	**GETTING WORSE** 88,18	
悪口 [warukuchi]	**BAD MOUTH,** **SPEAKING EVIL OF** 88, 16	
必見 [hikken]	**MUST-SEE** 89, 15	
特急 [tokkyū]	**LIMITED-EXPRESS TRAIN** 135, 89	

努力 [doryoku]	**ENDEAVOR** 90, 19
真空 [shinkū]	**VACUUM** 153, 91
空手 [karate]	(martial art without using any tools → **"empty hand"**) ↓ **KARATE** 91, 16
空白 [kūhaku]	**BLANK** 91, 12
島国 [shimaguni]	**ISLAND COUNTRY** 91, 39

電池 [denchi]	(*stored* **electricity**) ↓ **BATTERY** 92, 94
充電 [jūden]	**ELECTRIC CHARGE** 45, 92
電力 [denryoku]	**ELECTRIC POWER** 92, 19
電車 [densha]	**TRAIN** 92, 17
電気 [denki]	**ELECTRICITY** 92, 93

空気 [kūki]	**AIR** 91, 93
元気 [genki]	**HIGH SPIRIT, VITALITY** 21, 93
正気 [shōki]	**CONSCIOUSNESS, SANITY** 24, 93
人気 [ninki]	**POPULARITY** 12, 93
天気 [tenki]	**WEATHER** 13, 93

墓地 [bochi]	**CEMETERY** 146, 94	
基地 [kichi]	**(MILITARY) BASE** 146, 94	
土地 [tochi]	**LAND** 12, 94	
見地 [kenchi]	**VIEWPOINT** 15, 94	
名前 [namae]	**NAME** 80, 30	

配布 [haifu]	**DISTRIBUTION** 43, 82
友人 [yūjin]	**FRIEND** 84, 12
親友 [shin-yū]	**CLOSE FRIEND** 150, 84
支援 [shien]	**SUPPORT** 50, 84
一気 [ikki]	**AT A BREATH, IN ONE GO** 54, 93

一時 [ichiji]	**AT ONE POINT, TEMPORARILY, ONE O'CLOCK** 54, 133
四季 [shiki]	**FOUR SEASONS** 54, 140
特色 [tokushoku]	(**special color** that a thing has) ↓ **CHARACTERISTIC** 134, 76
文字 [moji]	**LETTER, CHARACTER** 50, 108
点字 [tenji]	**BRAILLE** 75, 108

赤字 [akaji]	**TO BE IN THE RED, DEFICIT** 76, 108	
治安 [chian]	**PUBLIC PEACE, PUBLIC ORDER** 112, 108	
安心 [anshin]	**PEACE OF MIND, RELIEF** 108, 16	
不安 [fuan]	**ANXIETY** 24, 108	
安否 [anpi]	**WHETHER ONE IS SAFE OR NOT** 108, 110	

証人 [shōnin]	**WITNESS** 111, 12
個人 [kojin]	**INDIVIDUAL** 114, 12
住人 [jūnin]	**RESIDENT** 115, 12
海外 [kaigai]	**OVERSEAS** 115, 30
海水浴 [kaisuiyoku]	**SEA BATHING** 115, 11, 123

不快 [fukai]	**UNPLEASANT** 24, 116
決心 [kesshin]	**DECISION, DETERMINATION** 116, 16
解決 [kaiketsu]	**SETTLEMENT, SOLUTION** 132, 116
決意 [ketsui]	**RESOLUTION** 116, 117
同意 [dōi]	**CONSENT, AGREEMENT** 21, 117

意外 [igai]
(better than or worse than your expectations)
↓
UNEXPECTED
117, 30

国境 [kokkyō]
COUNTRY BORDER
39, 118

心境 [shinkyō]
STATE OF HEART, STATE OF MIND
16, 118

教養 [kyōyō]
EDUCATION, SOPHISTICATION
128, 119

細胞 [saibō]
CELL
51, 120

飲食店 RESTAURANT
[inshokuten]

122, 47, 66

食欲 APPETITE
[shokuyoku]

47, 122

投資 INVESTMENT
[tōshi]

136, 123

資金 FUNDS
[shikin]

123, 12

金貨 GOLD COIN
[kinka]

12, 123

雑貨 [zakka]	**MISCELLANEOUS GOODS** 152, 123	
外貨 [gaika]	**FOREIGN CURRENCY** 30, 123	
特技 [tokugi]	**PROFESSIONAL SKILL, SPECIAL SKILL** 134, 126	
前者 [zensha]	**THE FORMER** 30, 127	
敗者 [haisha]	**LOSER** 128, 127	

役者 [yakusha]	**ACTOR, ACTRESS** 135, 127
教会 [kyōkai]	**CHURCH** 128, 27
教授 [kyōju]	**PROFESSOR** 128, 151
失敗 [shippai]	**FAILURE** 40, 128
政治 [seiji]	**POLITICS** 128, 112

山脈 [sanmyaku]	(a range of **mountains** runs like a *vein*) ↓ **MOUNTAIN RANGE** 10, 130
文脈 [bunmyaku]	**CONTEXT** 50, 130
子孫 [shison]	**OFFSPRING** 17, 131
終電 [shūden]	**LAST TRAIN** 131, 92
開始 [kaishi]	**TO BEGIN** 34, 112

正解 [seikai]	(**correct comprehension** of the question) ↓ **CORRECT ANSWER** 24, 132
同時 [dōji]	**AT THE SAME TIME** 21, 133
一等 [ittō]	**FIRST CLASS, FIRST ORDER** 54, 134
期待 [kitai]	(**waiting** for the *time* when a thing is realized) ↓ **EXPECTATION** 147, 135
役所 [yakusho]	**GOVERNMENT OFFICE** 135, 149

主役 [shuyaku]	**LEADING ROLE** 38, 135
攻撃 [kōgeki]	**ATTACK** 129, 136
自動 [jidō]	**AUTOMATIC** 52, 138
自動車 [jidōsha]	**AUTOMOBILE** 52, 138, 17
手動 [shudō]	**MANUAL OPERATION** 16, 138

一種	**A KIND OF**
[isshu]	54, 138

人種	**HUMAN RACE**
[jinshu]	12, 138

種子	**SEED**
[shushi]	138, 17

進歩	**ADVANCEMENT, PROGRESS**
[shinpo]	149, 140

全校	**THE WHOLE SCHOOL**
[zenkō]	37, 141

字幕	**SUBTITLE**
[jimaku]	108, 145
募金	**FUND-RAISE**
[bokin]	145, 12
基金	**FUNDS**
[kikin]	146, 12
前期	**FIRST TERM, PREVIOUS TERM**
[zenki]	30, 147
早期	**EARLY STAGE**
[sōki]	31, 147

思春期 PUBERTY

[shishunki]

51, 151, 147

期日 DUE DATE, DEADLINE

[kijitsu]

147, 11

近所 NEIGHBORHOOD

[kinjyo]

149, 149

住所 ADDRESS

[jūsho]

115, 149

台所

(**place** with a *counter* to serve)
↓
KITCHEN

[daidokoro]

26, 149

新車
[shinsha]

BRAND-NEW CAR

150, 17

青春
[seishun]

**YOUTH,
SPRINGTIME OF LIFE**

77, 151

親切
[shinsetsu]

(*gentleness* that *penetrates*)
↓
KINDNESS

150, 152

同情
[dōjō]

SYMPATHY

21, 154

友情
[yūjō]

FRIENDSHIP

84, 154

 **PUBLIC OPINION**

[seron]

 **QUARREL**

[kōron]

INDEX

In this index, the characters are arranged simply by the number of lines in the character, not by the number of actual strokes. For example, 口 (mouth) is categorized in "4 lines" in this index, but it is written with 3 strokes in proper orthography.

200

BIBLIOGRAPHY

Shinjigen 232nd edition. Kadokawashoten,
1985, Tokyo

Jōyōjikai. Shizuka Shirakawa, Heibonsha,
2003, Tokyo

The Kodansha Kanji Learner's Dictionary. Jack
Halpern, Kodansha International Ltd., 1999,
Tokyo